yukismart.com/b/6e8bd6

baby
เด็กทารก

dek tharok

boy
เด็กผู้ชาย

dekphuchai

friends
เพื่อน

phuean

girl
เด็กผู้หญิง

dek phuying

smile
ยิ้ม
yim

cry
ร้องไห้
ronghai

hair

ผม

phom

eye

ตา

ta

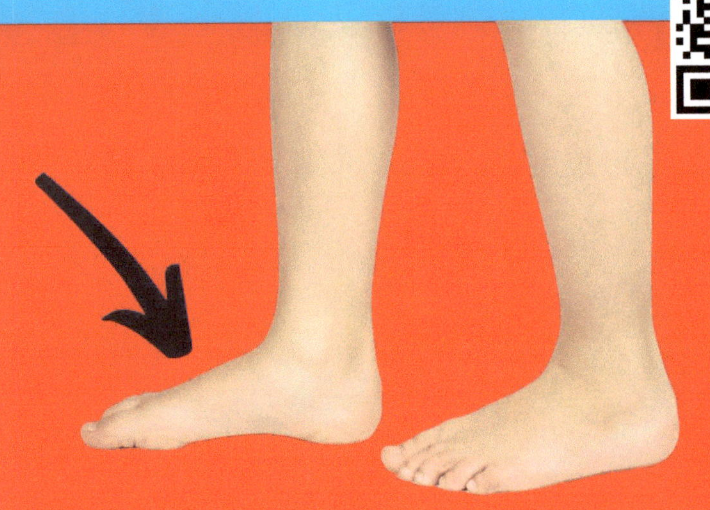

foot

เท้า

thao

hand

มือ

mue

nose
จมูก
chamuk

teeth
ฟัน
fan

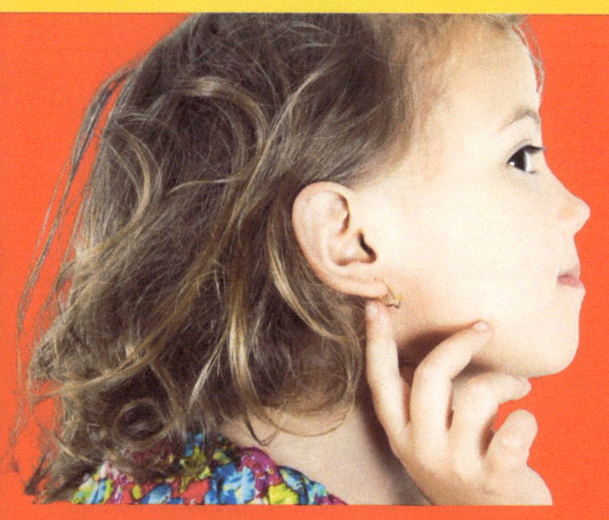

ear
หู
hu

tongue
ลิ้น
lin

sun

ดวงอาทิตย์

duang-athit

moon

ดวงจันทร์

duangchan

star

ดาว

dao

tree
ต้นไม้
tonmai

bird
นก
nok

coat
เสื้อโค้ท
suea khot

pants
กางเกงขายาว
kangkengkhayao

dress

ชุดกระโปรง

chut kraprong

shoes

รองเท้า

rongthao

red

แดง

daeng

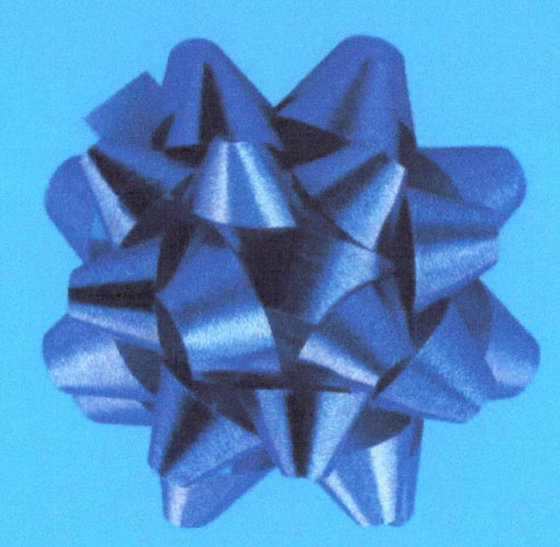

blue

ฟ้า

fa

yellow

เหลือง

lueang

pink

ชมพู

chomphu

white
ขาว
khao

green
เขียว
khiao

black
ดำ
dam

multicolored
หลากสี
lak si

rainbow

รุ้ง

rung

apple
แอปเปิล

aeppoen

banana
กล้วย

kluai

tomato
มะเขือเทศ

makhueathet

orange
ส้ม

som

carrot
แครอท
khaerot

peas
ถั่ว
thua

potato
มันฝรั่ง
manfarang

corn
ข้าวโพด
khaophot

lemon

มะนาว

manao

grapes

องุ่น

angun

pear

แพร์

phae

watermelon

แตงโม

taengmo

zucchini
ซุกินี
su kini

egg
ไข่

khai

mushroom
เห็ด

het

square
สีเหลียมจัตุรัส
siliamchatturat

circle
วงกลม
wongklom

rectangle

สี่เหลี่ยมผืนผ้า

siliamphuenpha

triangle

สามเหลี่ยม

samliam

cat

แมว

maeo

dog

สุนัข

sunak

fish

ปลา

pla

cow
วัว
wua

duck
เป็ด
pet

chick
ลูกไก่
lukkai

hen
แม่ไก่
mae kai

frog

กบ

kop

pig

หมู

mu

rabbit

กระต่าย

kratai

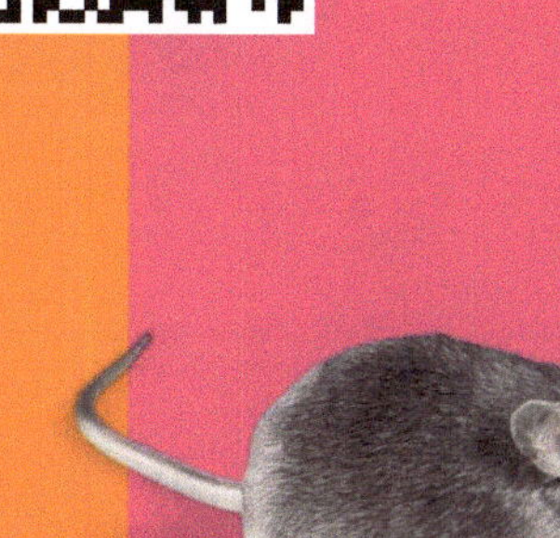

mouse

หนู

nu

horse

ม้า

ma

sheep

แกะ

kae

flower
ดอกไม้
dokmai

butterfly
ผีเสื้อ
phisuea

ladybug
แมลงเต่าทอง
malaengtaothong

snail
หอยทาก
hoithak

cake

เค้ก

khek

bread

ขนมปัง
khanompang

clock

นาฬิกา

nalika

key

กุญแจ

kunchae

book

หนังสือ

nangsue

ball

ลูกบอล

lukbon

table
โต๊ะ
to

plate
จาน
chan

chair
เก้าอี้
kao-i

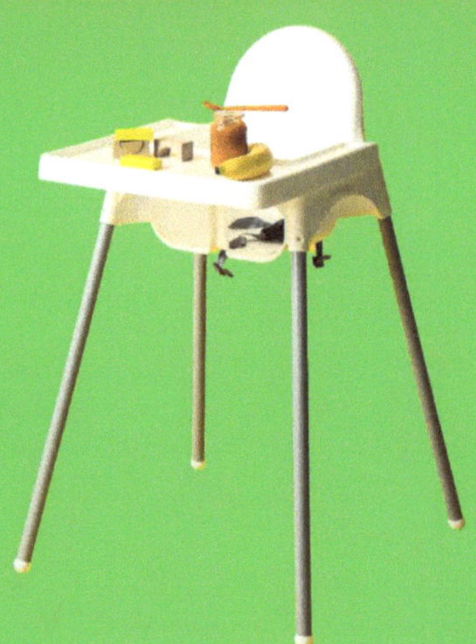

high chair
เก้าอี้สูง
kao-isung

fork
ส้อม

som

knife
มีด

mit

spoon
ช้อน

chon

cup
ถ้วย

thuai

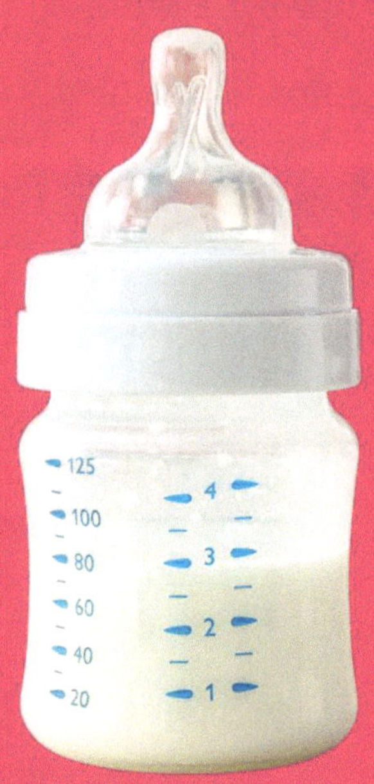

baby bottle

ขวดนม

khuatnom

glass

แก้ว

kaeo

bed
เตียง
tiang

crib
เตียงเด็ก
tiangdek

teddy bear
ตุ๊กตาหมี
tukkata mi

pacifier
จุกนม
chuk nom

towel
ผ้าขนหนู
phakhonnu

sink
อ่างล้างมือ
anglangmue

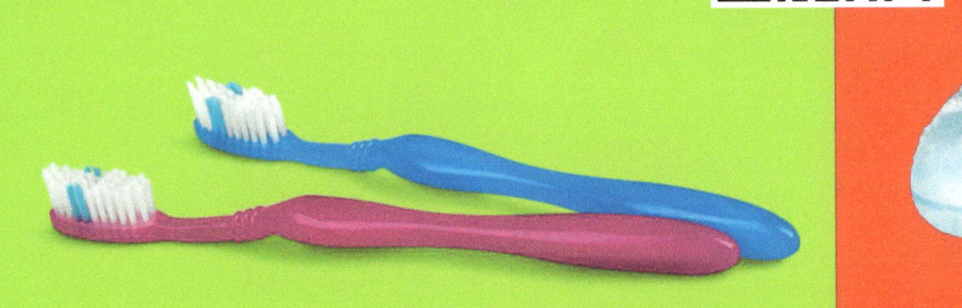

toothbrush
แปรงสีฟัน
praengsifan

soap
สบู่
sabu

toilet
โถส้วม
thosuam

potty
กระโถน
krathon

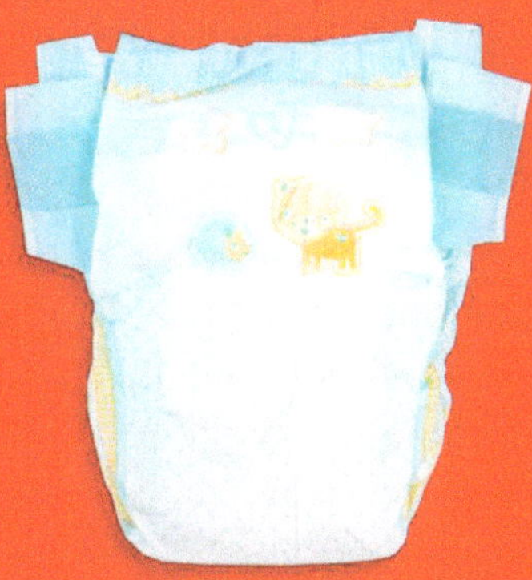

diaper
ผ้าอ้อม
pha-om

car

รถยนต์

rotyon

bike

จักรยาน

chakkrayan

plane

เครื่องบิน

khrueangbin

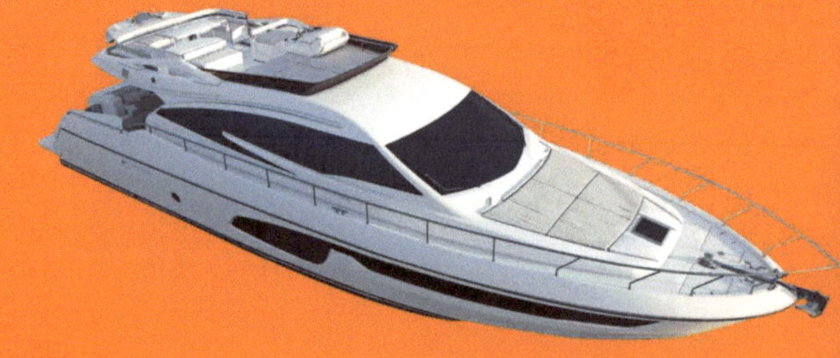

boat

เรือ

ruea

firetruck

รถดับเพลิง

rotdapphloeng

train

รถไฟ

rotfai

toys

ของเล่น

khonglen

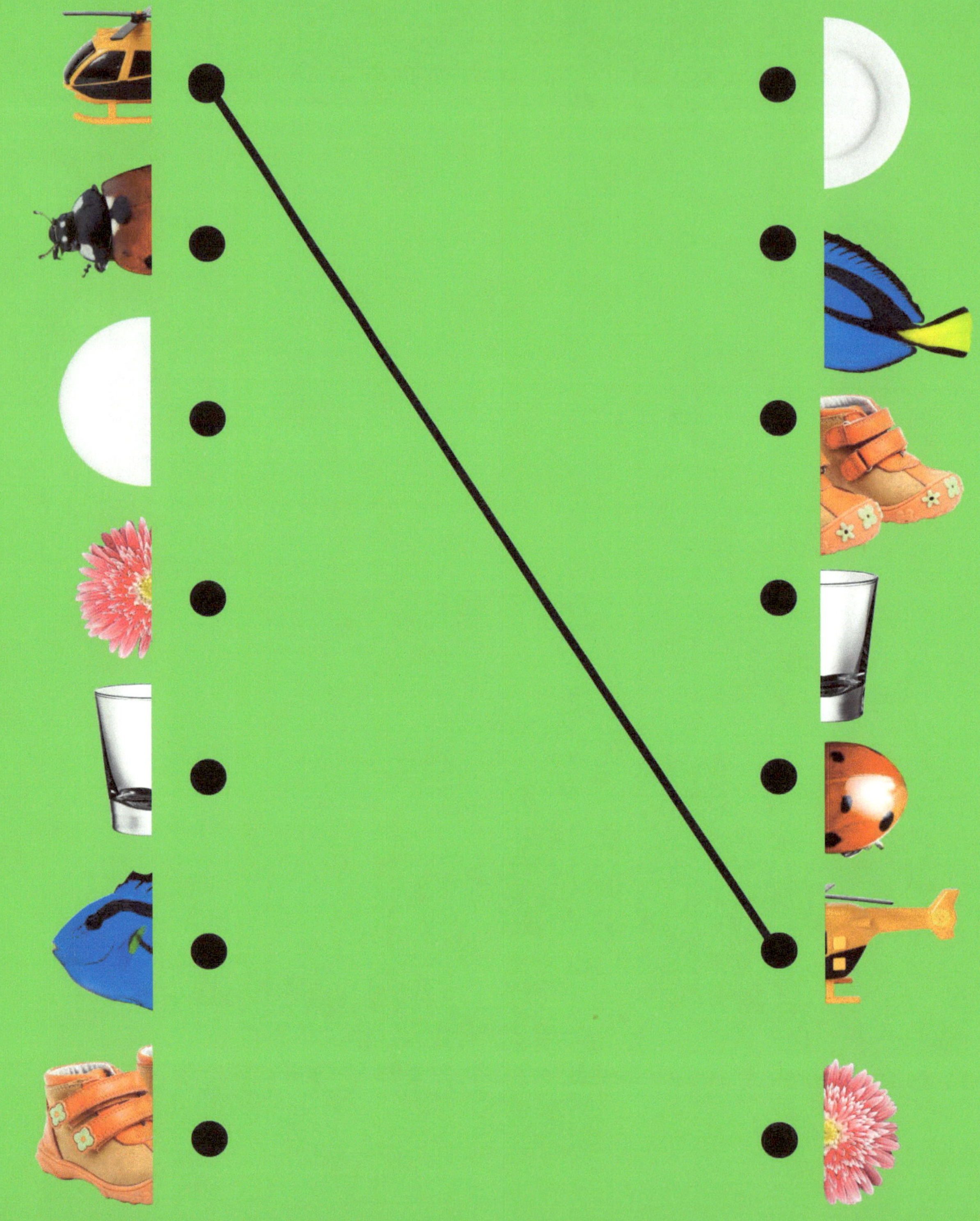